Days to P

MW00914254

Success in Life and Work Through Auto Hypnosis

Other Books by Stephen Hawley Martin:

Keys to the Kingdom and the Life You Want

How to Master Life
The Science Behind The Secret

A Witch in the Family
A Award-winning Author Investigates
His Ancestor's Trial and Execution

In My Father's House
An Award-winning Thriller

Death in Advertising
An Award-winning Whodunit

Success in Life and Work Through Auto Hypnosis

Workbook and Audio CD

**By Award-winning Author,
Stephen Hawley Martin**

THE OAKLEA PRESS

Richmond, Virginia

Thirty Days to Purpose and Prosperity
Success in Life and Work Through Auto Hypnosis

ISBN 10: 1-892538-38-5
ISBN 13: 978-1-892538-38-3

The Oaklea Press Inc.
6912 Three Chopt Road, Suite B
Richmond, Virginia 23226

Voice: 1 800 295 4066
Facsimile: 1 804 281 5686
Email: Info@OakleaPress.com

This book can be purchased online at
http://www.OakleaPress.com

Introduction

Congratulations! Purchasing the audio CD, *Success! Through Auto Hypnosis*, and this workbook was an excellent move. No doubt you made it because you want to get ahead. You want prosperity, abundance and your place in the sun. All this not only is possible, it will happen if you keep an open mind and follow the directions. As a Buddhist proverb says, "When the student is ready, the teacher will appear."

A more recent proverb says, "You'll see it when you believe it." This CD and workbook, used diligently and as instructed, will make you a believer in the power of your mind to bring you the life you want. And, as one of the great teachers of all time once said, "All things are possible for him who believes."

This workbook is laid out in seven steps, which have been divided into 30 installments or lessons to be covered one a day for the next 30 days. Each is meant to take only 10 or 15 minutes to complete. You can spend these few minutes any time during the day before you listen to the CD.

The first time you listen to the CD, however, I suggest that you do so at a time when you are not likely to fall asleep. This is so you will consciously know what you are listening to. After this playing, you should listen to the CD when you go to bed, at which time you are likely to fall asleep. And this is all right, because your subconscious mind will absorb what is being said and internalize the messages.

As the 30 days pass, a profound change in you will come about. After only a few playings, you will begin to feel invigorated and to experience a new sense of confidence, conviction and self-worth that you will welcome and enjoy.

Let me say, however, that some of the ideas and concepts this workbook and CD present may not coincide with what you have been taught to believe. Nevertheless, as one born into a family of skeptics and raised to believe in the scientific method, I have come to realize that these ideas and concepts are true. For a full understanding of why I've come to believe in these concepts—and for the logic, science and reasoning behind them—I urge you to read my book, *Keys to the Kingdom and the Life You Want* (Oaklea Press, 2002). It should answer questions this workbook may not.

STEP 1: *Understand who you are and why you are here*

Day 1:   Know the true nature of reality

Before physical reality existed, there was a unified force field that mystics call Spirit. Albert Einstein spent a good deal of his life trying to develop a formula to explain it. Today, we experience this field as the life force. If you have ever watched a time-lapse video of a seed germinating, pushing out roots and poking a stalk through the soil, you have witnessed the life force in action. It's what heals a wound, what animates every living thing. The life force is everywhere.

The life force is pure consciousness. It is the medium of thought. It can be seen in how a sunflower turns its head toward the sun even though it has no brain.

We are all connected to the life force; we, and everything in the universe, came from it. Mystics have long said that One Life underlies everything. The great Twentieth Century psychic Edgar Cayce said many times, "Spirit is the life, mind is the builder, and the physical is the result."

Experiments have proven that living things are connected by the medium of thought. Cleve Backster, an expert on polygraph machines (lie detectors), proved this by hooking up plants in his office to these machines. In one of many experiments he conducted, he had a machine randomly tip a cup of living brine shrimp into a pot of boiling water. The moment the shrimp hit the water, polygraphs attached to living office plants in three separate rooms, separated by closed doors, went wild.

In 1904, a man named Thomas Troward proposed a theory that explains how we as individuals create the circumstances of our lives. He called the underlying life force, the medium of thought, "First Cause." An individual's thoughts, Troward said, constitute "Relative Cause." They create what he called "prototypes" at the subatomic level. Left alone, these prototypes will eventually manifest in physical reality. Troward believed a person's circumstances are a manifestation of his thoughts.

To understand how this works, Troward said, we need to understand that there are two kinds of thought—lower and higher, or subjective and objective. What differentiates the higher from the lower is the recognition of self. A plant possesses the lower kind only. A human being possess both self-awareness and subjective mind.

What Troward called the lower mode of thought, the subjective, is the same thing I've been calling the life force. It supports and controls the mechanics of life, causing plants to grow and sunflowers to turn toward the sun. It's what made those office plants react when the brine shrimp were dropped into boiling water.

According to Troward, the conscious mind has power over the subjective mind that creates our reality. I discovered this firsthand in college when I learned to hypnotize others. I would put a willing classmate into a trance and tell him he was a chicken or a dog. Much to the amusement of my audience, he'd act accordingly. Why? Because his conscious mind had been bypassed and instructions given directly to his subconscious mind. This is how the CD will work when you are asleep. Instructions directing you to find purpose and prosperity will enter your subconscious mind unedited by your conscious thoughts.

Being totally subjective, the subconscious mind cannot step outside itself and take an objective look. The result is that the subjective mind is entirely under the control of the conscious mind and will work diligently to bring into reality whatever the conscious mind believes to be true.

The upshot of Troward's theory is that changing your thoughts and beliefs will change your life. But there are a couple of pitfalls you need to be aware of. First, the subjective thinks in pictures or images rather than in words. For this reason using the words "no," "not," "don't," or any negative form may have the opposite effect than what you intend. If, for example, you say to someone who is about to serve a tennis ball, "Don't double fault!" what is the image that's conjured up in his mind likely to be? That of himself making a double fault, of course. So what's likely to happen? He will double fault. His subjective mind thinks only "Double fault" because that is the image it has been given.

So always be sure always to frame your thoughts in a positive way. In the situation above, say, "Make this serve an ace!"

The other pitfall has to do with how the conscious mind is structured. It's divided into two parts: a conscious portion and an unconscious portion. The unconscious portion is programmed very much like a computer. For example, the first time you got behind the wheel to drive a car, you had to pay close attention to every detail. But over the years that you've been driving, your conscious mind made all the details part of you.

Everything you've come in contact with in this life is stored in your unconscious, including erroneous information. For example, as a child perhaps your parents said, "People in our family are cursed with a tendency to be overweight. All you have to do is look at food and it goes straight to your hips." Or perhaps, "Nobody in this family ever got rich. It's not meant to be." So in the unconscious part of your conscious mind today may be a belief that because you're a Jones or a Johnson or a Smith you're destined to struggle when it comes to money. But you aren't necessarily doomed. By bringing that information out of your unconscious, recalling where it came from, looking at it rationally and subjecting it to analysis, the erroneous beliefs can be erased.

The second bugaboo to look out for has to do with unconscious fears. These can usually be grouped under one of six headings: the fear of poverty (or failure), the fear of criticism, of ill health, of the loss of love, of old age and of death. The CD you are about to listen to will clear out old programming and rid you of these buried fears, while at the same time reprogramming your unconscious mind to direct you to find your purpose and to welcome prosperity into your life.

Exercise for the day

Reflect on the life force. Notice it in others and in other living things. Be thankful for it and feel it in your body, causing your heart to beat and your lungs to take in air. Your connection to the life force is your connection to good health and the One Life animating the universe of which you are a part.

NOTES:

_____

_____

_____

_____

_____

_____

_____

_____

_____

_____

_____

DAY 2: Understand why you arrived on the scene when and where you did

Whether or not you believe it, there was never a time when you did not exist, and there never will be. You are on what can be described as a journey. You are what might be pictured as a window on the life force. To understand this, it may help to think of yourself a cup submerged in the ocean. You are the cup, and you are the water within it, at one with and surrounded by infinite water. In this analogy, of course, the water is the equivalent of the life force. The cup shapes the water as your soul shapes the life force. You and the life force are one and inseparable. It has always existed and will always exist.

Your soul—the cup—has been evolving since life began. I and others who have studied metaphysics as well as the latest scientific research on reincarnation, believe that you have come into physical reality many times. The memory of your evolution could have been seen when your embryo unfolded in your mother's womb. It started as a fishlike creature, turned into a reptilian form with a tail and webs between fingers and toes, before it finally took human form. With each consecutive incarnation, you traveled up the evolutionary ladder, and your consciousness gained in quality and quantity. All through this time you were guided by the life force and subjective mind, just as schools of fish, flocks of birds, and animals such as antelopes and cheetahs are guided by subjective mind today.

As your consciousness and awareness grew, you began, gradually at first, to realize your separateness. Finally came the epoch, recounted in the story of Adam and Eve, when you became self-aware. You saw yourself as different, separate and distinct from other men and women and the rest of nature. It was as though you had eaten the fruit of the tree of the knowledge of good and evil. Unlike birds and animals of the forest or the savanna, you no longer relied solely on nature and instincts (subjective mind) to guide you. You believed yourself to be autonomous, and so you were. Your conscious mind could easily override intuition or instinct. As a result, you were able to make mistakes and, in a figurative sense, this meant you were banished from the garden and no longer walked with God in the cool of the evening.

The purpose of this workbook and CD is to help you find your way back, to help you get in tune with the One Life of which you are part. You are to become a conscious, rather than an unconscious, co-creator with the Universal Subjective Mind.

You have incarnated many times. The question before you is why did you incarnate in this place and time? The answer is that you had something to learn and something to accomplish. Perhaps you had what is known as karma to work out. (More will be said on this later.) Why did you choose the parents you chose?

Exercise for the day

Answer the following:

Where were you born? Why do you suppose that location is significant?

_____

_____

_____

_____

Think about your mother and father. What is special about them? Why do you suppose you chose them? What did they have to teach you? What trials did they put you through?

_____

_____

_____

_____

_____

_____

_____

_____

_____

Do you have brothers and sisters? You have probably incarnated with them before in significant relationships (as siblings, spouses, lovers). Do you have issues to work out with any? List them.

_____

_____

_____

_____

_____

_____

_____

_____

_____

_____

_____

_____

_____

_____

_____

Make plans to work out these issues. Write out your plan in brief.

_____

_____

_____

_____

_____

_____

_____

_____

_____

_____

Reflect on the situation of your family, the location of your birth, and the circumstances you were born into. Before you go to sleep tonight, before you listen to the CD, ask infinite intelligence to have you realize when you wake up tomorrow the significance of it all.

DAY 3: **Determine your talents**

Humans are like snowflakes. No two are exactly alike. We each have a unique combination of talents and abilities that enable us to serve others in ways no one else is quite able to do. Today's exercise is to spend some time investigating your talents.

When growing up, what did people tell you that you were gifted at or had a talent for, i.e., what were you always being recognized, admired, scolded or reprimanded for?

3

_____

_____

_____

_____

What did you do well growing up that seemed unusual or unique?

_____

_____

_____

_____

_____

What do you really like to do?

_____

_____

_____

_____

_____

What activity causes you to lose all sense of time?

_____

_____

_____

_____

_____

What are you doing when you hit a groove?

_____

_____

_____

_____

_____

What do you do that taps into some innate ability?

_____

_____

_____

_____

_____

What are you drawn to doing?

_____

_____

_____

_____

_____

What things do you pick up or learn to do much faster than others?
List them.

_____

_____

_____

_____

_____

What are you sensitive to and notice that others usually don't?

_____

_____

_____

_____

_____

What activity would you do if money were not an issue?

_____

_____

_____

_____

What can you do that you can't explain how you do it when asked about it?

_____

_____

_____

_____

_____

What activities appeal to you? Circle them in the following list:

Accounting	Sports	Massaging	Communicating
Building	Coaching	Organizing	Engineering
Counseling	Training	Performing	Inspiring
Designing	Selling	Sculpting	Listening
Fishing	Artistry	Singing	Meditating
Leading	Cooking	Supporting	Painting
Managing	Composing	Writing	Planning
Nursing	Dancing	Creating	Serving
Parenting	Encouraging	Acting	Studying
Plumbing	Healing	Caring	Teaching
Sharing	Learning	Coordinating	

Spend some time reflecting on your talents. What ability have you been blessed with?

Before you go to bed and listen to the CD, ask Infinite Intelligence to make clear to you when you wake up in the morning what your talents are and what you can become or already are an expert at doing.

Day 4:   Determine your temperament

Each person is unique. We want different things. Different things motivate us. We have different motives, purposes, aims, values, needs, drives, impulses and urges. And this is good. Imagine how boring life would be if everyone wanted the same things and thought the same way.

Though no one is exactly like you, there are other people who are similar. According to a widely used system of categorizing character and temperament types, 16 basic types exist. Determining which you fall into and the general characteristics of your type will help you better understand yourself. This will put you a step closer to finding your purpose.

4

The following questions are divided into four categories. Circle the letter for the answer that best fits your thinking and preferences. Be honest. There are no right or wrong answers. Which answer best describes you?

These questions will determine whether you give yourself an I or an E (circle one or the other for each):

○ E I like to go to social events and interact with lots of people, or
○ I   I would prefer to stay home and read a book or watch television.

○ E I like to know a little about a lot of things, or
○ I   I prefer to know a lot about a few things that really interest me.

○ E I usually hate to leave a party, my energy seems to increase as time passes, or
○ I I usually prefer to leave a party when I run out of steam.

○ E I like to keep up with what's going on with my friends, or
○ I I often get behind on what's going on with friends.

○ E People say I'm very approachable, or
○ I Sometimes people think I'm somewhat reserved and they hesitate to approach me.

○ E When the phone rings, I am usually the first to get it, or
○ I when the phone rings, I usually let someone else answer it.

Did you have more Es or Is? _____
(We'll discuss later what to do if it's a tie)

The next group of questions will determine whether you give yourself an S or an N. Again, there are no right or wrong answers. Be honest.

○ S I prefer to base my decisions firmly on experience, or
○ N I think hunches often pay off so I pay close attention to them when making a decision.

○ S I prefer to associate with sensible, down to earth people, or
○ N I like to be around really imaginative people.

○ S I'm more interested in what actually exists, or
○ N I'm usually more interested in what can be.

○ S When I do something, I normally do it the time-honored, usual way, or
○ N I often have my own way of doing things that works for me.

○ S I believe that facts are simply that—the way things are, or
○ N I believe that facts illustrate principles.

○ S I find so-called visionaries somewhat annoying, or
○ N I find visionaries rather fascinating.

Did you have more Ss or Ns? _____
(We'll discuss later what to do if it's a tie)

The next group of questions will determine whether you give yourself a T or an F. Again, there are no right or wrong answers. Be honest.

○ T I'm more impressed by principles, or
○ F I'm more impressed by emotions.

○ T I would rather people think of me as a logical person, or
○ F I would rather people think of me as a sentimental person.

○ T I'd say I'm more often a cool-headed person, or
○ F I'd say I'm more often a warmhearted person.

○ T When I make decisions, I feel more comfortable basing them on standards, or
○ F I feel more comfortable basing them on feelings.

○ T In judging others, I'm more likely to be swayed by principles, or
○ F I'm more likely to be swayed by circumstances.

○ T I'd say my head usually rules, or
○ F I'd say my heart usually rules.

Did you have more Ts or Fs? _____
(We'll discuss later what to do if it's a tie)

The final group of questions will determine whether you give yourself a J or a P. Again, there are no right or wrong answers. Be honest.

○ J I prefer to work toward a deadline, or
○ P I prefer to work without a deadline.

○ J I usually choose rather carefully, or
○ P I often choose rather impulsively.

○ J I prefer to be on time, or
○ P I'm often rather casual about time.

○ J I feel more comfortable once things are settled, or
○ P I feel more comfortable when things are open-ended.

○ J I like to have things planned out, or
○ P I prefer to let things happen.

○ J I'd say I'm more deliberate than spontaneous, or
○ P I'd say I'm more spontaneous than deliberate.

Did you have more Js or Ps? _____

Now write out the letters of your personality type. For example, my personality type is INTJ. Yours is _____.

Now go to Google on the Internet and enter your letters in the search engine—nothing more or less, just the letters. A number of sites will come up where you can read your personality profile.

If you had a tie between two letters, go back and take another look at the questions. If you have difficulty deciding which letter best describes you, you are likely a combination of two personality types. There's nothing unusual about this. Search both and read about both. Decide which is the closest or best description of you. Perhaps it is indeed a combination.

NOTES:
_____

_____

_____

_____

_____

_____

_____

_____

_____

_____

_____

_____

_____

_____

_____

_____

_____

_____

_____

_____

_____

NOTES:

STEP 2: *Clean out the attic of your mind*

So that you can begin anew, you'll need to clean out the attic of your mind. Chances are there's a lot of stuff up there that's not doing you any good. By this I mean, get rid of buried fears, erase past karma, forgive emotional debts, and dissolve destructive bonds. By jettisoning what's holding you back, you can move ahead faster. Most of us have a lot of stuff piled up in our unconscious minds and souls, sapping our strength, draining off spiritual and emotional energy that might otherwise be put to work on our behalf and on behalf of others. The CD will help you get rid of this, but so will consciously bringing it to the surface, having a look and tossing it in the trash.

DAY 5: Break the bonds that tie you to the past

The baggage to unload today falls into the category of destructive attachments you may have, and feelings of guilt about your own past actions.

Let's start with attachments. The first thing for you to do is forgive. Forgive yourself and forgive others. Both love and hate make bonds. Bonds of love can be good. Bonds of hate are always destructive.

List those against whom you are holding a grudge:

_____

_____ 5

_____

_____

Now, one at a time, picture each person in your mind and tell them you forgive them. Mean it. This may seem difficult to do, but holding onto hate and bitterness toward someone will cause you a great deal of harm. Remember the Law of Attraction. You attract to yourself what's in your mind. So clear away the bad stuff.

If you are in an abusive relationship, get out of it. Get out of it and forgive the abuser. This may be easier said than done, but what can possibly be gained by holding on to the person or to negative feelings? If you hold on to bitterness, it will come back to you. So forgive. Pray for the one who has abused you. Pray that God's peace, serenity and love will come to them.

Perhaps your parents pushed you in a direction you didn't want to go. Even though it might have happened long ago, it may still be having a negative effect on you. What possible good can it do to hold on to the feelings? Today is the first day of the rest of eternity. Don't perpetuate a bond that eventually will have to be worked out—if not in this lifetime, then another. Dissolve it. Forgive.

Now it's time to forgive yourself. Almost everyone has done things they are ashamed of and would just as soon forget about. But usually they can't forget—not until they forgive themselves.

If you did someone a wrong turn, if at all possible, seek that person out and apologize. Ask their forgiveness. If that's not possible, picture them in your mind. Ask forgiveness.

If you believe in God, ask God's forgiveness, too. Many believe, and rightly so, that if they are truly sorry and ask God's forgiveness, they are forgiven.

DAY 6:   Overcome the fear of failure

Now you know about the six basic fears. The CD has been helping you erase them by instructing your subconscious mind to allow them to be washed away with the purple colored liquid. For the next few days, you will take an objective look at them and then jettison each from the attic of your mind.

The fear of poverty or failure comes first because in many ways it can be the most debilitating. It is self-fulfilling, since the fear itself can bring poverty or failure about. For example, are you a procrastinator? An underlying fear of failure is probably the root cause and can be counted upon to produce failure.

Are you overly cautious? Do you see the negative side of every circumstance or stall for the "right time" before taking action? Do you worry that things will not work out, have doubts—generally expressed by excuses or apologies—about whether you'll be able to perform? Do you suffer from indecision that leads to someone else or circumstances making the decision for you?

Are you indifferent? This generally manifests as laziness or a lack of initiative, enthusiasm or self-control.

If so, realize this and then let go of this fear that it is most certainly holding you back. Just let it go. Let it wash away with the purple-colored liquid.

Whether you're a CEO or a sixteen-year-old, the only thing you truly have absolute control over is your own thoughts.

You may say, I can't control what thoughts pop into my head. True. You may not control what thoughts come to you, but you can decide whether to discard a thought or keep it. Whatever thoughts you hold on to will expand and eventually manifest.

Beginning now, each time you catch yourself with a negative thought, a thought that says "I can't," "it's not possible," "maybe someone else but not me," get rid of it.

NOTES:

_____

_____

_____

_____

_____

_____

_____

_____

_____

_____

_____

_____

DAY 7:   Overcome the fear of criticism

If you suffer from fear of criticism, it probably resulted from a parent
or sibling who constantly tore you down to build himself up. You'll
know this is a problem if you are overly worried about what others
might think, if you lack poise, are self-conscious or extravagant.

Why extravagant? Because of the urge within you that says you
need to keep up with the Joneses. You must rid yourself of inner
voices and urges that tell you to think even twice about what others
will say. Simply push them out of your mind.

Let's think for a minute about the fear of criticism. There have
been places and times in history when what others thought was
worth worrying about. My great, great, great, great, great, great,
great grandmother, Susannah Martin, for example, was accused
of being a witch and hanged in Salem, Massachusetts, in 1692.
I've written a book about this called *A Witch in the Family* (Oaklea
Press, 2006). She was a proud woman who did not suffer fools
well, and she was independent-minded. After her husband died,
she was able to run the farm successfully without a man around.
Think of the talk this caused in the Puritan community where
people generally believed women weren't capable of such things.
To them it was impossible without witchcraft.

The opinions of Susannah Martin's neighbors mattered a great deal.
They led to an unpleasant and untimely death.

What about today?

There are still countries in the world where you might have to watch out what your neighbors think or what the "thought police" hear about you, but in most developed countries this simply is no longer a valid concern. What others think or don't think of you is their problem, not yours. Yet worrying about what they think can cause you a great deal of unhappiness and keep you from pursuing your purpose.

I once had a friend who ignored his intuition and went through with a marriage because he felt it was too late to turn back. The invitations had already been sent when he began to feel a sense of impending doom. But he went through with it because he was worried what people would think and say. Can you imagine the pain he brought himself and his bride? He lived with her about year and then went through an unpleasant and very expensive divorce.

He allowed the fear of criticism to cause him and his bride a great deal of pain. Don't let it do the same to you. Allow it to be washed away with the purple-colored liquid.

DAY 8:   Overcome the fear of ill health

Have you ever noticed that people who talk about illness, worry about illness, are preoccupied with this or that possible illness, think they feel a pain here or there or that they were exposed to some germ, are precisely those who stay sick most of the time? The power of suggestion is at work. So to rid yourself of the fear of ill health, it should be enough to know that what you worry about and think about eventually will happen.

Consider this. When you walk through a shopping mall or an airport, the number of germs floating in the air and resting on surfaces such as door handles, table tops and railings is incalculable. Practically every disease known to man is present. Yet, the vast majority of people do not get sick. Why? Because they have what doctors call an immune system that recognizes and takes action against foreign substances, including viruses and germs, that do not belong in the body.

But what if the immune system is turned off? Your mind can flip the switch in either direction. Research into the placebo effect, for example, shows that a person's thoughts can have a profound effect on the body. Patients are given sugar pills that they are told are real medicine. Invariably, some percentage of these patients will experience the effects that real medicine would be expected to bring about. The percentage of those cured by placebos often matches or exceeds the percentage of those cured who took real medicine—proof positive that the mind can heal.

Whenever thoughts or worries of ill health enter your mind, shoo them away. And tonight, when you listen to the CD, allow the purple-colored liquid to wash them away forever.

NOTES:

_____

_____

_____

_____

_____

_____

_____

_____

_____

_____

_____

_____

_____

DAY 9: Overcome fear of the loss of love

Fear of the loss of love manifests itself as jealousy and is self-fulfilling like the others. Everyone needs some space. When you are jealous, the person you are trying so hard to hang on to feels smothered, with the result that you end up pushing that person away.

Give them love, but give them room. It they leave you, they would have done so anyway. You can now move on to a truly meaningful relationship.

Jealousy can also hurt you in business and in other endeavors such as sports or social situations. Perhaps this is why envy is one of the Bible's seven deadly sins and not coveting is one of the Ten Commandments.

An alternative translation of the word "sin" is "error." It's an error or mistake to envy or be jealous of another, because this sets up a condition in the mind in which the person of whom you are jealous has what you want, and you do not. As long as this condition exists in your mind, it will also exist in reality.

Push thoughts and feelings of jealousy away. Give people room, give them love, and love will be returned to you. And tonight, when you listen to the CD, let the purple-colored liquid carry away all thought and fear of the loss of love.

DAY 10:   Overcome the fear of old age

Today, you will dispense with the fear of old age. This fear is closely aligned with the fear of ill health and the fear of poverty, because these are the conditions a person really is concerned about, deep down. The power of suggestion is at work here, too. If you think you're too old to do this or that, you will indeed be too old.

Consider this. My eight-year-old son is the same flesh and blood as my wife and me. I saw him when he was born, still connected by an umbilical cord. In fact, I clipped it myself. My wife was thirty-six at the time; I was fifty-four. Yet the cells in my body, and in my wife's body, and in my son's body all were the most recent in an unbroken chain of cell division that went back to the first life on earth. All the cells—my wife's, my son's, and mine—are at the end of a chain that is precisely the same age: billions of years.

As noted before, "Spirit is the life. Mind is the builder. The physical is the result." The cells of the body age—the telomeres at the end of each cell that connect them to other cells get shorter and shorter each time they divide—because people think they should look and feel older as the years go by.

When you've learned all you can from this life, the time will come for you to check out. And check out is what you will do. No one says you have to look old, feel old, or be old.

Tonight, allow the fear of old age to be carried away with the purple-colored liquid.

46

DAY 11:   Overcome the fear of death

Now we've come to that final bugaboo, the fear of death. As with the other fears we've disposed of, there is, in Franklin Roosevelt's words, "Nothing to fear but fear itself." Consider the millions who have had near-death experiences and are no longer afraid to die. A number of books, including what may be the original by Raymond Moody called Life After Life, are filled with the testimony of people who were pronounced clinically dead and then resuscitated. These people report they were greeted by guides as well as by loved ones who have gone before. They now look forward to being bathed once again in the all-encompassing light, which many have described as total, unconditional love. In essence it was as though, when they died, they were returning home after a long and sometimes difficult journey.

But wait a minute, you say. "I'm like Woody Allen. I'm not afraid to die, I just don't want to be there when it happens." Then take heart. Most who have returned from the dead say they do not expect to experience pain when it happens again. It has been reported by many that the spirit exits the body the instant it looks as though death is inevitable.

And only a small handful who have had hellish experiences worry about what they may encounter in the nonphysical world. These folks need to know what you know—that each of us creates his own reality. We experience what we expect to experience, what we think we deserve. In the physical world, this takes time. In the nonphysical world of spirit, which is the medium of the mind, we instantly create our reality, just as we do in dreams. If we expect Hell, the Hell we believe we deserve is the Hell we will get. If we expect Heaven, our vision of Heaven is what we will have.

Tonight, allow the purple-colored liquid to carry away the fear of death.

NOTES:

_____

_____

_____

_____

_____

_____

_____

_____

_____

_____

_____

_____

_____

NOTES:

_____

_____

_____

_____

_____

_____

_____

_____

_____

_____

_____

_____

_____

_____

_____

_____

_____

_____

_____

STEP 3: *Identify your mission*

DAY 12: What do your life experience and your temperament suggest you should do?

To determine your ideal job or profession, review your notes from Days 2 and 3 about the circumstances of your birth and your talents. Look again at the list of activities, and make sure you identified those that appeal to you. (See page 26.)

Now spend some time on the Internet reading about the characteristics of your personality type, which you determined on Day 4.

Plug in your letters and do a Google search. Review your profile on several different web sites. See which famous people have the same personality profile as you. What are these people known for? Keep looking, and find out what jobs typically appeal to someone with your profile. If you don't find a page, try this phrase, "Careers for (your four letters) Personality Types." Write down the jobs and professions that strike a chord.

12

_____

_____

_____

_____

_____

_____

Look back at Days 2 and 3 (pages 17 through 26). Consider the circumstances of your birth and what you experienced growing up. Think about your talents. Add to this what you have been trained to do in school, by the work experience you have so far in life and the activities that appeal to you. Which one of these jobs or professions makes sense?

_____

_____

_____

_____

_____

Is it anything like what you're doing now?

If so, keep at it. If not, is this something you can aspire to in your current job or place in life? What would you have to do to change course and follow a path to this destination?

_____

_____

_____

_____

_____

_____

If a change is called for, what would you have to do to make the change? Don't dismiss this out of hand. I have a brother in-law who quit his job as a mechanical engineer at the age of 36 and went to medical school. Now, at 42, he's finishing his residency. Such things are possible, but you must realize you have to start the journey where you are now. If you have obligations, it may not be practical for you to quit your job and head off in a new direction. But perhaps there is a way to begin—either as a hobby, or by taking courses in night school, or by moonlighting or volunteer work—that will start you on the way. Write this down.

_____

_____

_____

_____

_____

_____

Before you start the CD tonight, ask for guidance. Ask Infinite Intelligence to show you a direction to take to lead you to a life of purpose. Tomorrow, when you wake up, stay alert. Chances are that sometime during the day, either through intuition or perhaps because of something you read or see or hear, guidance will come.

DAY 13:   Understand the hero's journey

Today I'm going to share something I've experienced myself that was life-altering. When you really want something and remain attentive, an opportunity to pursue it will appear. The late Joseph Campbell labeled this, "The call to adventure." This call will come whether the desire you hold is known to you on a conscious level or whether it's hidden in the subconscious. Having completed this workbook to this point, I suspect it may now actually be at a conscious level in your case.

When the call comes, you will be presented with a choice. You can follow your adventure and gain from it. Or you can refuse the call, in which case you will stagnate.

You need not take my word for this. Myths throughout the ages tell the same tale. Refusal of the call converts what otherwise would be positive and constructive into negative form. If a would-be hero refuses to take the opportunity presented, he or she instead becomes a victim bound by boredom, hard work or even imprisonment. In the myth of the Minotaur, for example, King Minos refused the call to sacrifice the bull, which would have signified his submission to the divine. He didn't know that this would have resulted in his elevation to a higher state. So, like a modern-day business executive or professional, he became trapped by conventional thinking and attempted to overcome the situation through hard work and determination. Indeed, he was able to build a palace for himself, just as many executives and professionals today build mansions in the suburbs. But it turned out to be a wasteland, a house of death, a labyrinth in which to hide and thus escape from the horrible Minotaur.

And look at what happened to Daphne, the beautiful maiden pursued by the handsome Greek god Apollo. He wished only to be her lover and called to her, "I who pursue you am no enemy. You know not from whom you flee. It is only for this reason that you run." All Daphne had to do was submit, to accept the call, and beautiful and bountiful love would have been hers. But as you may know, she did not submit. She kept running and as a result turned into a laurel tree, and that was the end of her.

Let me tell one more story. It is the same one as the two above, and conveys the same warning. This time it comes from Jesus. It can be found in all three synoptic Gospels. This account is from Mark 10:17-23, the New International Version (NIV) translation:

> *As Jesus started on his way, a man ran up to him and fell on his knees before him. "Good teacher," he asked, "what must I do to inherit Eternal Life?*
>
> *"Why do you call me good?" Jesus answered. "No one is good—except God alone. You know the commandments: 'Do not murder, do not commit adultery, do not steal, do not give false testimony, do not defraud, honor your father and mother.'"*
>
> *"Teacher," he declared, "all these I have kept since I was a boy."*

Jesus looked at him and loved him. "One thing you lack,"[1] he said. "Go, sell everything you have and give to the poor, and you will have treasure in heaven. Then come, follow me."

At this the man's face fell. He went away sad, because he had great wealth.

Jesus looked around and said to his disciples, "How hard it is for the rich to enter the Kingdom of God!"

The disciples were amazed at his words. But Jesus said again, "Children, how hard it is to enter the Kingdom of God! It is easier for a camel to go through the eye of a needle than for a rich man to enter the Kingdom of God."

If ever a person received the call to adventure, it was this rich man. If he answers the call, he will start on the road to doing what he was meant to do, learn and grow as a follower of Jesus. As with Minos and Daphne, the promise is that he will develop and eventually experience the ecstasy of a relationship with the divine. But first, as was the case with them, he must give up his earthly treasure. Like the other two before him and many of us today, he was much too attached to his earthly wealth to do so.

I believe that what Jesus called the Kingdom of Heaven or God is a state of being that can be achieved here on Earth when you do

---

[1]The first law is, "Put no other gods before Me." The rich man had done this by making money his number-one god; e.g., it was the "one thing he lacked."

what you came here to do, allow the life force to flow through you, and use your talents to serve others. Often, it is frightening to take that first step toward it, to answer the call. It's a journey I have taken, so I know this from experience. I won't bore you with a detailed account of sleepless nights. Suffice it to say I had to fight my own dragons and demons and to confront the fears that told me I ought to cling to what I had rather than fly to what others regarded as pie in the sky. But, as in any hero's adventure, when the going got really tough, unseen hands, the support of the divine, stepped in, and I made it through. My advice is never give up, no matter how tough the going gets. As the old saying goes, it's always darkest before the dawn. But rest assured, the dawn will come. If you want more reassurance, I advise you to read my book, *Keys to the Kingdom and the Life You Want*, in which I tell my own personal story.

Expect the call. Be on the alert.

DAY 14:   Write down your mission

One intent of this workbook and CD is to lead you to an understanding that you are much more than your physical body. The truth is, your physical body is very much like a raincoat that you wear on this trip to Earth. When the trip is over, you will take it off. But you will still be you.

Many creation myths as well as people who are regressed through hypnosis to the time of their origin as individual beings indicate that human souls were created to be companions with their Creator. They further say it is the Creator's desire that we willing choose to be a companion and co-creator. (Who would want a friend who has been forced to be so?) Your soul or higher self is your connection. If you have not yet gotten in touch with this aspect of the One Life, it is time to begin a dialog with what in 1 Kings 19:11-12 is called "the still small voice." This is done by spending quiet time each day and by welcoming the still small voice into your life. It is important to actually extend the invitation, by the way, so you have to ask.

Then what? Some people meditate. Others, like me, simply take a long, solitary walk each day. If you keep at this, sooner or later it will lead to a shift in your consciousness. You'll realize you are not alone; that higher guidance is always available. Once this happens, your conscious mind and your subconscious mind will begin to form a partnership. As they start to work in harmony, your life will continually change for the better, and your sense of fulfillment will grow. Abundance eventually will follow.

Right now, spend a few minutes in quiet meditation. Clear your mind. If thoughts come to you, push them away. Perhaps say the word "one," silently or out loud, to push them away. Do this for several minutes.

Now, while your mind is quiet, invite the Still Small Voice to come to you. Ask it what your calling is.

Write down what comes.

_____

_____

_____

_____

_____

_____

_____

_____

_____

_____

If nothing comes, or if what comes is not clear, ask again before you go to bed and turn on the CD. In the morning, fill in the first thought comes to you.

NOTES:

NOTES:

STEP 4: *Identify your ideal*

Perhaps you have now identified your calling and
have determined to pursue it. Now it's time to
establish your ideal.

DAY 15:   Establish your ideal

As in the early days of sailing on the ocean, it is important to have a marker, such as the North Star or the Southern Cross, to guide your way. This means you must identify an ideal that is personal to you and set your compass by it.

A true story is told in *The Edgar Cayce Handbook for Creating Your Future*, written by Mark Thurston and Christopher Fazel (Ballentine Books, 1992). While in college, a man named Jerry attended a weekend seminar called "Preparing for the Future." Included in the seminar was a workshop that involved writing down in as much detail as possible just what he would like to be doing in twenty years. Jerry gave this exercise serious attention and did his best to visualize an ideal day twenty years into the future. By a curious coincidence he found that envelope almost to the day twenty years later. As he read over the old document, he was amazed to discover that he was now actually living his projected scenario with uncanny accuracy.

Was Jerry a psychic who successfully predicted the future? I don't think so. More likely, what happened illustrates something deeper and more profound, a principle articulated over and over in the psychic readings of Edgar Cayce: Mind is the builder. In other words, with the awesome power of your mind you can create your future, your situation in the world, even the very person you are.

You may be able to fool some of the people all of the time and all of the people some of the time, but you cannot fool the universe.

What's in your mind is going to be reflected back to you, and that means you'd better have good stuff in there. It means having an ideal that goes beyond the accumulation of wealth alone. In fact, wealth should not be your end goal. Wealth should come about as a byproduct of what you want to do with your life. This suggests your ideal should incorporate a quality or state of being you admire that complements your life purpose.

What are your personal values? What do you hold as an ideal? Many individuals have difficulty even understanding these questions. Why? Because most people let unconscious motives and values drive their thinking. These ideals lie hidden, like the workings of a software program that mysteriously makes things happen on a computer screen. For most of us, beliefs and values are so embedded in the cultural atmosphere around us that we don't even recognize or see them. It's like trying to observe the air we breathe. But the time has come to bring them out into the open.

Spend a few minutes meditating on these qualities:

Love, Gentleness, Kindness, Self-Control, Brotherly Love, Patience, Fellowship, Mercy, Selflessness, Truth, Hope, Persistence, Faith, Joy, Humility, Justice, Peace, Obedience, Humility, Harmony, Understanding, Grace, Honor, Contentment, Abundance.

Which of them resonate with you? Which would like to develop more fully? I suggest you combine these into a statement of your ideal. Put this down on paper.

For example, my ideal is to employ brotherly love, humility and persistence as I impart understanding that helps others find peace, harmony and abundance.

It may help in formulating this ideal to think of someone alive today, or perhaps someone who lived in the past, who embodies your ideal. For example, it might be Jesus, Moses, Mother Teresa, Harry Truman, Theodore Roosevelt, Thomas Jefferson, Abe Lincoln or Mahatma Gandhi. It may be someone from the list of famous people who have the same personality type as you.

One web site says Thomas Jefferson had the same personality type I have. Perhaps it's not surprising, then, that I have long looked up to Jefferson and found him to be a source of inspiration. If you can identify someone who inspires you in this way, it will help keep you on track to regularly remind yourself of him or her—perhaps read and get to know more about that individual—as you move forward in life and pursue your goals.

My ideal is:

_____

_____

_____

_____

A role model and source of inspiration to me is:

_____

_____

_____

_____

NOTES:

_____

_____

_____

_____

_____

_____

_____

_____

_____

_____

_____

_____

_____

_____

_____

_____

_____

_____

NOTES:

_____

_____

_____

_____

_____

_____

_____

_____

_____

_____

_____

_____

_____

_____

_____

_____

_____

_____

STEP 5: *Take responsibility*

By now you know that your personal reality is a
reflection of what's in your mind. It is inevitable,
then, that those who consider themselves victims
will always be victims. Until they take responsibility for their own lives, the circumstances of
their lives will be dictated by others.

DAY 16:   Understand that failure is an illusion

I once was a partner in a very successful advertising agency that had as its motto, "Don't be afraid to fail." The creative director of that agency had a huge poster made with those words on it, and he put it up on a wall of the creative department. He was looking for cutting-edge stuff from his staff, and when you try to do cutting-edge stuff, sometimes it isn't going to work.

But the motto and the poster did work. They created a freethinking atmosphere that led to some really innovative advertising that caused that agency to become regarded as one of the most creative in the world. For example, if you've seen the commercials with the GEICO caveman, you've seen one of that agency's campaigns.

16

I have to say the people in that advertising agency were not a particularly philosophical bunch. They were much more interested in creating advertising that would get noticed and call attention to a client's selling proposition than in pondering the mysteries of the universe. That's why, perhaps, they would not have understood if I had told them that—depending on your point of view—there is no such thing as failure.

How can that be? Well, take the example of Thomas Edison. He wanted to invent a light bulb. For the light bulb to work, it had to have a filament that glowed when electricity ran through it. That wasn't a big problem. The problem was finding a way and the right material to use for that filament to glow and to keep glowing and glowing without burning up after a few minutes. Edison finally invented one that lasted 1500 hours, but legend has it that it took 10,000 tries before he got it right.

A newspaper reporter is said to have once asked him what it felt like to have failed 10,000 times. Edison is quoted as having said, "If I find 10,000 ways something won't work, I haven't failed. I am not discouraged, because every wrong attempt discarded is often a step forward."

My mother told me often, "If at first you don't succeed, try try again." If you view each time something doesn't work as a learning experience, rather than failure, this won't be so difficult or frustrating as it otherwise might be. As I say on the CD, in every setback is the seed of success. You have to learn from it and apply what you learned. Albert Einstein defined insanity as, "Doing the same thing over and over again and expecting different results." So, like Edison, figure out why it didn't work and try again.

You may have heard about the skeletons that were found in the desert near the crest of a sand dune. On the other side was an oasis. If the men who died there had crawled a few more feet they'd have seen the oasis and been saved. Think about that next time you are tempted to quit.

Take a few minutes, and list the things you've done in your life that you once thought were failures.

_____

_____

_____

_____

_____

_____

_____

_____

Now consider them in a different light. Write down what you learned from them.

_____

_____

_____

_____

_____

_____

Tuition at elite universities seems high, but what you learn can be invaluable. The same is true of experiences in the school of life.

DAY 17: Realize that "like creates like"

We've been thinking a lot about the Law of Attraction. The fact is, there are a number of laws that stem from or are related to this, and most people don't know them because they aren't taught in ordinary schools.

As you take responsibility for your life and circumstances, it will help to know and understand these laws. Today we will cover "like creates like," the first law of metaphysics.

Jesus said it was possible to know a man by his fruit. An apple tree cannot produce oranges. What sort of fruit have you produced so far in life? Look around you.

17

The message is that you must change yourself if you wish to change your outer circumstances. That's what the CD and this workbook are about. Chances are you have already made great strides. At this point in this workbook, your outward circumstances probably already are changing. Notice the differences.

Our attitudes, feelings and actions determine the attitudes, feelings and actions of others toward us. This makes each of us responsible for the kinds of relations we have. So if we don't have the sort we want, we need to work on ourselves. This is a powerful realization. Each of us determines how others behave toward us by the way we treat others. If we dislike others, others will dislike us. If we are kind to others, others will be kind to us. If we are considerate of others, others will be considerate of us. If we are hateful, others will be hateful. The list could go on indefinitely. Our motives create like motives in others. Our emotions, like emotions; attitudes, like attitudes.

Having realized this, spend a few minutes and list the changes in yourself that you have already made since starting this workbook.

_____

_____

_____

_____

_____

_____

Now list those changes you still need to make.

_____

_____

_____

_____

_____

_____

Day 18: Realize that "we receive what we give"

This is a sub-law of Like Creates Like. In the East it is called the Law of Karma. It's the law Jesus had in mind when he said, "Do not judge, or you too will be judged. For in the same way you judge others, you will be judged, and with the measure you use, it will be measured to you." (Matthew 7:1-2)

If we give love, love will come back to us. If we hate, hate will be returned. Usually, the specific person for whom we feel love or hate will return it. But this is not always so. Nor will a specific act on your part necessarily come back to you in precisely the same form. What you can count on over time is that what you have given out will be returned to you. As in Newtonian physics, the universe seeks balance. Equilibrium may take years to achieve. It may take lifetimes, but it always is achieved.

But, and this is a big "but," contrary to popular belief, karma is *not* a form of punishment. Karma is a way we can learn. Once you have learned the lesson, once you have forgiven yourself and have forgiven others, the boomerang will not return. When you truly understand the futility of holding a grudge, of trying to get back at someone or of judging others, you will break the cycle by no longer engaging in such things.

Some people believe in reincarnation, others don't, and it really doesn't matter if you do for this workbook and the CD to help guide you to a better life. But research by a University of Virginia professor and psychiatrist, the late Ian Stevenson, MD (October 31, 1918 - February 8, 2007) strongly indicates reincarnation, which billions of people believe in, is a fact. Many people I know, having discovered this, have a desire to be regressed through hypnosis to learn what they did in past lives that may be holding them back in this one. I'm curious about past lives, too. But I do not believe that—except perhaps in a few extreme cases—regression therapy is actually necessary. I'm certain that at one point or another you and I have done just about everything bad, and good, that can be imagined. But I know, and I hope you now know, that it is possible to start anew, without having to go through the trauma of an "eye for an eye and a tooth for a tooth." Meditation, study and reflection can lead to a higher level of consciousness that, combined with true repentance and forgiveness of yourself and others, can wipe out negative karma. This is one of the Jesus' key messages.

The realization that we are all part of One Life, that we can't hurt others without also hurting ourselves, triggers the Law of Grace. Grace dissolves the need for a karmic boomerang. We have overcome the faulty thinking and lack of compassion that lead to wrongful action and now are able to start anew. Grace is a very real phenomenon. You can read more about it in my book, *Keys to the Kingdom.*

You belong here on this earth because you are a child of the universe, a part of the whole. You have a role to play. Drop that old baggage, move forward and accept the life you came here to lead.

DAY 19: Realize that "our intentions determine the outcome"

I said it before, you can sometimes fool yourself and others, but you can't fool the universe. According to the Law of Intention, two people can perform the same act, yet each can get the opposite result. For example, both could bake a cake to surprise a friend, each thinking the friend will like it. Their basic intentions, however, might be quite different. One might act in the spirit of love, wanting to bring the friend joy and happiness. The other might act in the spirit of selfishness, hoping to impress the friend in order to gain attention or favor. Each may perform the same act, baking a cake for a friend, but the fruits from the act will be different. One will bring love, the other a hypocritical response.

Before you act, ask yourself, "What is my intention in this action? Is it in line with my ideal? Am I being sincere? Am I free of hypocrisy, deceit or duplicity?"

If your purpose is in the flow with peace and love and the ideal you have set out for yourself, benefits will flow to you naturally.

Think about this. Oprah Winfrey has said she did not set out to become one of the richest women on earth. That was not her intention. Her intention was to become the best talk show host she could possibly be.

Spend some time in thought considering your intentions. Do they line up with your ideal? Or do you have work to do?

Write out what you intend for others as a result of the work you would like to do.

_____

_____

_____

_____

_____

_____

_____

_____

_____

_____

_____

_____

_____

_____

DAY 20: Realize that "like attracts like"

Another sub-law of Like Creates Like is Like Attracts Like. We are most attracted to people who are like ourselves—with similar beliefs, ambitions, and values. The old saying, "Birds of a feather flock together" is true.

As you grow and change, you will find that the people around you will change. This is probably happening to you already as a result of this workbook and CD. Don't worry about this. If you are no longer comfortable in the company you keep, it is time to move on.

Also consider how you dress, groom yourself, your personal manners and your way of speaking. Is this how others you would now like to be around present themselves? Is it how others present themselves who are doing what you aspire to in life?

List the changes you plan to make in how you present yourself.

_____

_____

_____

_____

_____

_____

DAY 21: Realize that "when we seek, we find what we need"

Here's an anecdote to illustrate this law.

Some time ago, I watched a "Biography" episode on A&E Network, the subject of which was Adam West, the actor who became famous in the Sixties playing Batman. When the show was canceled, West found he was now typecast and had great difficulty landing other acting jobs. He was reduced to doing shopping mall openings and other promotions. In one for Lear Jet, he had posed with the founder of that company and his lovely young wife from Switzerland.

A few years later, West was in Italy shooting a spaghetti western. Recently divorced, he learned that Lear and his wife also had divorced, and that the ex-wife was living in Geneva. West remembered being quite infatuated with her and became determined to find her. Even though he had no idea where in Geneva she lived, or even what last name she now went by, West went to Geneva. He wandered around the city, going nowhere in particular. Before long, he and the woman he was seeking came upon each other on the street. Eventually, they were married. This was not a coincidence. West had been earnestly seeking, and he found that which fulfilled his search.

This law works unfailingly, provided what is being sought in is line with and will advance the life mission of the seeker. Edgar Cayce, for example, once used his psychic ability to pinpoint the location of oil on a claim in Texas. Much later, it was proven the oil actually was there, but at the time one obstacle after another, in the form of mishaps and equipment problems, hindered the work of the drilling team. Finally, the team of wildcatters he'd hired gave up, and Cayce lost his investment. But he learned something important. He came to the realization that his psychic abilities were a gift to be used for the good of humankind, and not for his or anyone else's personal gain.

This law was demonstrated to me constantly when I was writing my first book of nonfiction, a book now out of print, which had to do with my own personal spiritual awakening. I would reach a point where I'd get stuck. I'd need an example to illustrate a point, perhaps a quotation, or maybe a little-known fact from history or science, but I'd have no idea exactly what I needed, much less where to look. This was before the Internet was in wide use and before Google had been invented. So I'd get in my car and drive to a bookstore or a library and go to a shelf or section that seemed right. I'd pick out a book, open it at random, and two times out of three, my answer would be on that very page. Seldom was it necessary to look in more than one or two books.

What do you need that will advance your life mission? Write down what you need. Seek it. Ask that you find it.

_____

_____

_____

_____

_____

_____

_____

_____

_____

_____

_____

_____

_____

_____

_____

_____

_____

_____

Begin soon to seek whatever it is, and you will find it.

DAY 22:   Realize that "the fault you see is the fault you own"

It's a fact that traits in others that cause us to become upset would not rile us if we did not possess the same or something similar. What we are seeing is a shadow side of ourselves that needs to be brought into the light and acknowledged. Jesus said, "How can you say to your brother, 'Let me take the speck out of your eye,' when all the time there is a plank in your own eye? You hypocrite, first take the plank out of your own eye, and then you will see clearly to remove the speck from your brother's eye." (Matthew 7:4-5) Jesus was able to see what most of us cannot. Faults that we react to the most in others are the very faults we need to deal with ourselves.

An excellent book that includes much on this is *Awakening the Heroes Within: Twelve Archetypes to Help Us Find Ourselves and Transform Our World* by Carol S. Pearson (HarperOne, 1991). It's one of the few books I've read twice, in this case with about ten years between readings, and I benefited from it both times. Once you finish the 30-day path you are on now, which I believe will result in a quantum leap forward, I hope you will want to keep up your studies and continue to grow. If so, this may be one book to consider.

Every one of us has facets we keep hidden, often from ourselves as well as others. Knowing this puts you in position to grow. You see, we are each composites of the archetypes—the twelve characters who embody specific characteristics such as warrior, magician, child, sage, destroyer, orphan, fool and so forth. Each of these archetypes has a positive and a negative, or "shadow," side. We all have some of each of them in us. If we keep the shadow side of an archetype hidden, if we do not acknowledge it, this shadow will assert itself in some way and will very likely get us in trouble.

What are the traits or qualities in the various people you know that bug you the most? List them.

_____

_____

_____

_____

_____

_____

_____

_____

_____

Resolve to recognize these in yourself. You don't have to banish them. Just realize they are there and make peace with them. Your recognition of them will bring them under control.

DAY 23: Realize that "the best outcome always results"

When I hear people say that everything happens according to God's plan, or that all is happening "just as it should," I have to shake my head. This flies in the face of the fact that we have free will on the physical plane. People often act from base or selfish motives and make bad choices. Fear and hatred can lead people to do horrendous things. Individuals die or suffer harm because they ignore their intuition, or the "still small voice" of higher consciousness.

It is naive to think that natural disasters or that a misguided person or group exercising free will do not sometimes lead to trouble and sorrow that might have been avoided. Bad things indeed happen to good people. But here's the good news. The law stated above, also known as the Law of Grace, says that no matter how bad a tragedy may be, the best outcome possible will come from it.

The cliché, "Behind every cloud is a silver lining," is true. A father who lost his daughter in the Columbine incident, for example, now spends his time crisscrossing the continent speaking to high school students about the need we all have to develop our spiritual side and to recognize that we are part of something far larger than ourselves. Reportedly, his efforts have had a positive effect on thousands. I'm willing to bet that many teen suicides have been prevented by his words and by the passion he feels about his faith and his daughter's death. Columbine remains a terrible tragedy. Nothing will change that. But if it had not happened, the teens who have been helped would not have heard that father's words.

My advice is this: When something bad happens, try not to dwell on it beyond a normal period of time needed for grieving. As quickly as possible, start looking for the good that will come from it. There will be some good. The silver lining will appear. At the very least, it will be a learning and growing experience. At best, it can lead to opportunities you never dreamed possible.

Think about something bad that happened to you in the past. You may still wish it hadn't happened, but think about it. Hasn't some good come from it, too? Write down what happened and the good that came about as a result.

_____

_____

_____

_____

_____

_____

_____

_____

_____

_____

_____

_____

_____

_____

_____

_____

_____

_____

_____

_____

This shows the life force (God, if you prefer) at work. The life force is the opposite of entropy, which is the force that causes things to break down and deteriorate. The life force pushes in the other direction, toward growth and evolution. It supports and lends a hand to each of us as we strive to unfold and become all we can be. In the case of Columbine, the free will of those boys resulted in a terrible tragedy. Nevertheless, a bad situation has been used by that father to bring good to many others.

DAY 24: Realize that "as you believe, so is it for you"

A sub-law of the Law of Attraction is that that our beliefs manifest in our lives. This will happen even if we are not consciously aware of what we believe about a given topic. The phenomenon of belief creating reality was explained by Edgar Cayce's source, who said, "As thought, purpose, aim, and desire are set in motion by our minds, their effect is a condition that is." In other words, if a person believes it, it already exists—perhaps not yet on the physical plane, but on the mental plane. What exists on the mental plane needs only time before it manifests on the physical. As you recall, "mind is the builder and the physical is the result."

24

It follows that if we are to transform our lives, we must change our beliefs. What may make this difficult is that most of us are not aware at a conscious level of all that we believe. Many of our beliefs are the result of unconscious programming. So we often create our lives from beliefs that we don't recognize and can't recall.

But this does not have to continue, because clues to your beliefs are all around you. I have a female acquaintance, for example, who continues to attract men who turn out to be, as she says, "no good." What should this be telling her? I suspect one of two possibilities. She may think that men in general are "no good." Or perhaps she doesn't believe that she has what it takes to attract anything other than men who are no good. Either way, her belief leads to a self-fulfilling result, so she needs to change it. The same thing is behind problems such as recurring financial difficulties, less than productive relationships with coworkers, or poor health and illness.

People used to think, for example, that sitting or sleeping in a draft would cause a cold. Today we know that colds are caused when a virus penetrates the immune system. If we believe that drafts cause colds, it follows that our immune system is going to be more likely to allow a cold virus in when we are forced to sit or sleep in a draft. The belief is self-fulfilling and leads to the result.

Our beliefs have perhaps the most profound effect on our lives when it comes to our belief in God, or the lack of it, and in the nature of the God we believe in. If we don't believe in God and assume there is no rhyme or reason to human existence, this will be our experience. If we believe that God is a jealous God and punishes us for our transgressions, this will be our experience. If we believe that God is forgiving—in effect a loving, forgiving Father who wants what's best for us, as Jesus indicated was the case—this will be our experience.

The truth is, God does not judge us. We judge ourselves.

God is the life force, the opposite of entropy, the universal subjective intelligence that underlies and gives rise to physical reality. Our conscious minds are an extension of this. We have a conscious mind and an unconscious mind that contain everything we have learned or experienced in this lifetime. We also have a subconscious mind that contains everything we have learned or experienced in our many lifetimes, another name for which is the soul. This joins with the subconscious minds of all other humans and ultimately blends into universal intelligence, which by nature is subjective because it is everywhere at once. It cannot possibly think outside itself and thereby consider things objectively. In other words, it cannot make value judgments. As Jesus said, "[God] causes His sun to rise on the evil and the good, and sends rain on the righteous and the unrighteous." (Matthew 5:45)

But we humans can and do make value judgments. And when we do, we are sending those thoughts into the universal subjective mind to which we are connected. This goes to work to reflect them back to us, thereby creating the reality and experience we expect and believe are coming to us, based on the God we believe in.

What about you? Do you believe in God? _____

If so, what is the nature of the God you believe in? Is He a wrathful God? A loving, forgiving God? Or is He an uninvolved God, even a nonexistent God, leaving things up to chance?

_____

_____

_____

_____

If you believe in a loving, forgiving, protecting God, I suggest you hold on to that belief, but also realize that the universe works by the laws we are studying. If you do not believe in a loving God, or don't believe in God at all, I suggest you adopt the belief that the universe works strictly by laws, including the laws of physics and the metaphysical laws we have been discussing. This includes the Law of Grace covered yesterday.

DAY 25: Realize that "life is the experience of your choices"

The final law puts your fate squarely in your own hands. In the Earth School, you have free will. You can choose what thoughts to keep and which to reject. You can choose your beliefs. You can choose to go to class, study and work hard, or you can decide to cut class, guess at the answers, and take your chances. You can also choose to "follow your bliss," as Joseph Campbell advised his students, to ask for divine help, and trust the Law of Grace will work to bring it to you.

The gift of free will means you can create the life you want by the choices you make. I'm talking about big choices and the little choices you make throughout the day. Choices about whether to take a job for the money or a different one that's more satisfying because it allows you to use your talents to help others and follow your ideal. You can choose whether to forgive, or to hold a grudge. You can choose whether to stop, think, trace your anger to its cause and change yourself, or whether to take the easy way and blame the other person.

What are some of the unfortunate choices you have made in your life?

_____

_____

_____

_____

_____

_____

_____

_____

_____

_____

_____

_____

What are some of the good choices?

_____

_____

_____

_____

_____

_____

_____

_____

_____

_____

_____

_____

_____

What choices are you facing?

_____

_____

_____

_____

_____

_____

_____

_____

_____

_____

_____

_____

Based on what you now know, what are the right choices?

_____

_____

_____

_____

_____

_____

_____

_____

_____

_____

_____

NOTES:

_____

_____

_____

_____

_____

_____

_____

_____

_____

_____

_____

_____

_____

_____

_____

_____

_____

_____

NOTES:

STEP 6: *Develop your sixth sense*

Guidance is always available to you in the form of
what most people call intuition. This is information
coming through to you from your subconscious
mind, which is in touch and in tune with the universal subjective mind and the subconscious
minds of others. The next few nights will cover
how to improve your intuition.

DAY 26:   Realize that ESP and intuition are real

Some people use intuition and don't even know it. If the second
letter in your personality profile is an "N," it means you are an intuitive type. Gut feelings and patterns of consistency are important
guidance for you. At some point in studying a problem, things seem
to snap into place and further study is no longer necessary. You
have your answer. On the other hand, if your second letter is an "S,"
you are likely to discount intuition and rely more on experience
to guide you. You are likely to seek out and study much more data
than your "N" counterpart would before you feel comfortable
making a decision.

No matter what your personality type, I believe anyone can develop
intuition. The first step is to not allow yourself to make snap judgments and to remain open to new possibilities. Most people suffer
from what might be called preconceived-idea syndrome. They look
at a situation and pigeonhole it. But chances are they may be putting
some of what they see and encounter into the wrong pigeonholes.

The trick in seeing reality as it really is, as well as in transforming
your life, is not to react immediately to whatever you may encounter.
This is true when it comes to developing intuition and to changing
unwanted habits. You see, there's a small gap between the time
something happens and when you react to it. Use that gap to reflect
and stop yourself from reacting. In other words, think twice, check
for intuitive signals, and deprogram yourself in situations where
your normal reaction might not have been productive. For example,

if you are watching your weight, don't just automatically eat that piece of cake simply because it is put before you. Think, "A moment on the lips, forever on the hips," and politely turn it down.

Believe you can use the gap to develop intuition and break those habits. As you know now, our beliefs create our reality. If you think intuition is a bunch of hooey, that it doesn't work—that will be your experience. This was demonstrated on national television in study aired on the Discovery TV Channel. Two researchers conducted the same ESP experiment in the same laboratory using the same equipment. A great deal of effort was exerted to keep everything identical, except one. One researcher believed ESP was valid, and the other did not. Both tests were supervised by impartial observers, including the Discovery Channel TV crew.

The experiment employing the researcher who believed in ESP had a statistically significant number of correct scores, which meant the experiment was a success. ESP was demonstrated scientifically to be real. But the number of correct hits in the experiment employing the doubting Thomas researcher fell within parameters that could be accounted for by chance. So this time the experiment failed to demonstrate the validity of ESP. Apparently, the one and only variable—belief—made the difference. The first researcher believed, and the second didn't. Each got the result he believed he would.

Reflect on times you seemed to get information through some source other than the senses of sight, hearing, smelling, tasting, touch, or hearing. For example, have you ever heard the phone ring and had a hunch it was someone, or had a mental picture of the caller, even through there was no particular reason for him or her to call you at that time?

_____

_____

_____

When you walk into a room, or step onto an elevator, do you sometimes feel eyes on you, turn to look, and notice someone quickly look away?

_____

_____

_____

Have you ever had the feeling someone close to you needed your help and you called them or went to them and found out this was true?

_____

_____

_____

If you said yes to any of these, you've received information through your sixth sense.

DAY 27: Be aware of ways intuitive information can come to you

Not everyone receives intuitive insights or messages in the same way. I usually experience them as feelings in the area of my solar plexus, as mentioned in yesterday's lesson. But some hear voices.

I remember a time when people were sure that hearing disembodied voices meant a person was crazy. That's why people who hear them usually don't say so—unless they are crazy. But I have friends I'm pretty certain are not crazy who receive intuitive messages in the form of spoken words all the time.

It's probably the case that just about everyone has internal voices. The trick is to distinguish between them. Many are likely to be old tapes of what you were told by your parents, teachers, or others in authority when growing up. They may not have given you good advice, so don't mistake these voices for intuition. If whatever you are receiving says you "should" do something, or if it puts a guilt trip of some kind on you, it is not intuition. Good advice or information from the universal mind is never manipulative. And when you follow it, if it was truly intuition, you'll feel light, more alive. You'll have energy. Remember this, because in the future, even after you've made a big, life-changing decision, you'll experience this same sense of buoyancy if you are truly following direction from your subconscious mind. On the other hand, if you are off course, you'll feel drained, blocked, maybe even somewhat depressed. If you experience such feelings, I suggest you reconsider your decision.

Another way messages are received is called psychic vision, or clairvoyance. This is a form of ESP that expresses itself as a picture, symbol or visual impression. Traditionally, it is associated with receiving visual insights that come either through meditation or in dreams. You probably are aware of psychics who help police by visualizing the scene of the crime or the location of a body. You may have had experiences with clairvoyance and not realized it.

Answer the following:

Have you ever had a mental image of something, perhaps in a dream, and what you saw actually happened? _____

Have you ever experienced a voice, mentally, that gave you information or advice that turned out to be correct? _____

Do you sometimes have a feeling or a "knowingness" about something that turns out to be accurate? _____

DAY 28: Learn to entrain your mind

Sometimes intuition will come in loud and clear. This usually happens in life-changing or life-threatening situations, such as when a driver feels a powerful urge to slow down or pull off to the side of a winding road just before a car appears, screeching around the upcoming curve on the wrong side of the road. A friend of mine tells the story of seeing his future wife presented at a dance. He knew her but not very well. What sounded like a voice outside him said, "Here comes the mother of your children." These sorts of things do happen, but usually, and this is almost always true for me, it's necessary to get into the right frame of mind to get intuitive messages. This normally involves what's called entraining the mind.

What is meant by entraining the mind? According to my dictionary the word entrain means "to pull or draw along after itself; to go aboard a train, or to put aboard a train." But the way I mean this word is different. Earlier I mentioned different levels of mind—conscious, unconscious, personal subconscious, shared subconscious and universal subjective subconscious. Actually, I left some out for the sake of simplicity. There are seven of them according to the College of Metaphysics in Windyville, Missouri. Contained within these levels of mind, which we are all connected to and share, is everything known to man or woman, past, present, and possibly future. So, theoretically, all you'll ever need to know can be found within your own mind. The trick is allowing it to find its way into your conscious mind. That's where entrainment enters in. You need to get those levels of mind all lined up like the cars of a train, so the information you need flows from one car to the next until it reaches the engine that's your conscious mind.

I use several techniques to do this. Meditation is one. There are a number of ways. One is to sit quietly, back straight, feet on the floor, and relax. I push away all monkey-mind thoughts and ask my higher mind a question. Then I simply wait patiently and enjoy the silence. Whenever what I recognize as another monkey-mind thought enters my mind, I simply push it away.

What's a monkey-mind thought? It is mind static such as, "Did I remember to turn off the oven?" Or, "I wonder what's for lunch today?" Or, "Man, oh man, that report is due tomorrow. I'd better stop this and get on it." Eventually an idea or thought will come to me that is germane, but if one does not after ten minutes or so, I'll go on to something else, confident that eventually what I need to know will be revealed.

28

Often I will ask the question again when I go to bed at night, and the answer will come the next morning or sometime during the day— although sometimes, when I am particularly eager for an answer, it will come to me in the middle of the night. For this reason, I always keep a pen and some paper by my bed.

Frequently, however, the answer will not come directly into my mind. It will come from outside and can arrive from anywhere. But I will know when it appears because of a feeling I get in my gut like the bass string of a viola being being plucked.

Perhaps the most common way for me to entrain my mind is to take a long walk, usually for about forty-five minutes. I do this almost every day for the exercise and because it is my quiet time. Sometimes there will be a question I'm wrestling with, and at other times there won't be anything specific on my mind. There's something about being out in nature that opens the channel to the inner levels of my mind. Others have told me this is true for them as well.

Is there something on your mind? Tonight, when you go to bed, ask about it. Try to put the question in the form of a yes or no answer. Either you will have your answer in the middle of the night (don't forget to have pen and paper handy), as soon as you wake up or during the day. Be alert. It could come from within, or it may come from an external source, such as something you read or hear. Become conscious of the feeling you get when the answer comes. Remember that feeling, and put more trust in it each time the information you receive proves to be accurate.

DAY 29: Review the steps to developing your intuition

Today, consider and reflect on the steps to developing your intuition:

1 **Believe intuition is real.** Laboratory tests have demonstrated that scientists who don't believe in intuition cannot replicate experiments that have been successfully conducted by scientists who do.

2 **Realize that humans spend a lot of time in denial.** We don't recognize the truth because it may be too painful or might force us to change our beliefs. So before you dismiss new information, ask yourself if you have evidence to back up your dismissal.

3 **Understand that the truth cannot hurt you.** It may ruin your day, but in the long run it will set you free.

4 **Ask for guidance and be open-minded.** "Ask, and it will be given."

5 **Entrain your mind through meditation.** Your mind consists of layers. You must align them so that information can flow from the deepest sources up to conscious awareness.

6 **Go past "old tapes" in order to hear the true voice of intuition.** These recorded voices are parents or former teachers: "You should do this, you shouldn't do that." Intuition has serenity, a peacefulness to it that never tries to manipulate. Learn to recognize the difference.

7 **Finally, look for consistency when insights come.** Do they meet the facts or fly in the face of them? Look closely. And be honest with yourself.

NOTES:

_____

_____

_____

_____

_____

_____

_____

_____

_____

_____

_____

_____

_____

_____

NOTES:

_____

_____

_____

_____

_____

_____

_____

_____

_____

_____

_____

_____

_____

_____

_____

_____

STEP 7: *Maintain balance in your life*

We've come to the end of our time together in this workbook, and you are almost ready to set out to conquer your field of endeavor, but there's one last, important step to cover.

DAY 30: Learn to give equal time to the three parts of you

I'd be surprised if you do not now have a pretty good idea where you are headed and the next steps to take on your journey.

Once you find your purpose, and begin the work you came here to do, you may become so absorbed in it that you lose yourself in activities related to it. Tonight's final lesson is to realize that in your present form, you are made up of three components: body, mind, and spirit. All require attention. To ignore any one is to risk illness. In order to maintain good health, the body requires regular exercise and a balanced diet, the mind needs stimulation, and the spirit must be nurtured.

I believe that much physical as well as mental illness in our society can be traced to a lack of spirituality. I urge you to continue your studies in this regard. And if possible, join some sort of group made up of people who have a similar world view. The fellowship of like-minded people is important and will boost you up and give you energy.

And remember, no matter how successful you are in your work, true contentment and abundance will elude you if your success comes at the expense of your body, your peace of mind, your home, your marriage, or your children. We all have a tendency to become overzealous about one aspect of life and allow the others to go wanting. This is why we need to take an inventory frequently of our daily and weekly activities.

Answer the following:

What regular exercise routine do you have?

_____

_____

_____

Do you eat wholesome foods, consuming them in moderation?

_____

_____

_____

What do you do regularly to stimulate yourself mentally? (Such as read, play Bridge, take classes, do crossword puzzles, et cetera)

_____

_____

_____

Who are the important people in your life?

_____

_____

_____

_____

Do you spend adequate time with them?

_____

_____

Are you part of a spiritual fellowship group?

_____

_____

_____

List the changes you need to make to bring your life into balance.

_____

_____

_____

What physical changes, i.e., in diet and exercise?

_____

_____

_____

What in the area of mental stimulation or exercise?

_____

_____

_____

What do you need to do to continue your spiritual growth?

_____

_____

_____

_____

_____

_____

_____

_____

_____

_____

_____

_____

_____

_____

_____

_____

NOTES:

_____

_____

_____

_____

_____

_____

_____

_____

_____

_____

_____

_____

_____

_____

_____

_____

_____

NOTES:
_____

_____

_____

_____

_____

_____

_____

_____

_____

_____

_____

_____

_____

_____

_____

_____

_____

_____

NOTES:

_____

_____

_____

_____

_____

_____

_____

_____

_____

_____

_____

_____

_____

_____

_____

_____

_____

_____

NOTES:

_____

_____

_____

_____

_____

_____

_____

_____

_____

_____

_____

_____

_____

_____

_____

_____

_____

_____

NOTES:

Hear Stephen Hawley Martin on the Radio

Award-winning author Stephen Hawley Martin hosts a radio show each week on www.WebTalkRadio.net called The Truth About Life. Join him there as he digs into and unravels life's mysteries—such as what happens when we die? Is there proof of reincarnation? Does Satan exist? Is there a Hell? What is the life force? What about spirit possession? What is the true purpose of life? How can we harness the power of belief? Are there really ghosts, and if so, what are they?

Listen to what the experts he interviews have to say, then decide what's true—because the truth will set you free. After all, the more we know about life, how and why it works, the better able we will be to make it work for us.